Praise God from whom all Blessings Flow.

A BIBLICAL THEOLOGY
OF THE HOLY SPIRIT

Dear Rev. Howard,

    Thank you so much for the encouragement and prayers you so graciously gave in the writing of this Book.

    May God richly bless you forever and a day.

        With much Love;

          Sincerely,

          Rev. Mr. Iota M. Mitchell

A BIBLICAL THEOLOGY OF THE HOLY SPIRIT

Rev. Dr. Ida M. Mitchell

iUniverse, Inc.
New York Lincoln Shanghai

A BIBLICAL THEOLOGY OF THE HOLY SPIRIT

iUniverse books may be ordered through booksellers or by contacting:

iUniverse
2021 Pine Lake Road, Suite 100
Lincoln, NE 68512
www.iuniverse.com
1-800-Authors (1-800-288-4677)

Scriptures quoted from the King James Bible, unless stated.

ISBN-13: 978-0-595-39928-4 (pbk)
ISBN-13: 978-0-595-84317-6 (ebk)
ISBN-10: 0-595-39928-2 (pbk)
ISBN-10: 0-595-84317-4 (ebk)

Printed in the United States of America

Contents

Introduction

Theology is a widely used term. Therefore, it is necessary to identify more closely the sense in which it is being used in this document. Biblical Theology in this document is based upon the faithful to the teachings of the Bible. Biblical Theology is the Holy Spirit is a study of the Spirit of God throughout the Old and New Testaments of the Bible.

Theology is derived from two Greek words, theos and logos, theos meaning "God" and logos meaning "speech" and "doctrine". The doctrine covered in this document is not exhaustive, but with hope will bring honor and glory to God the Father and to his Son Jesus Christ.

This doctrine of the Holy Spirit is also being written on the premise that it will appeal to common readers and lay persons, as well as seminarians and theology students. This is an attempt to explore the Scriptures, give more knowledge and broaden the understanding of all individuals concerned and obtain accurate and infallible information concerning who the Spirit of God is and the functions of the Holy Spirit.

It is a well-founded and frequent complaint by those concerned that the subject of the Holy Spirit has been avoided by Theologians. The reason being that is the most controversial of all doctrines. The Spirit of God is intangible and difficult to visualize. God the Father is understood fairly well because the figure of the father is familiar to everyone. The Son is not too hard to conceptualize, for he actually appeared in human form, and was observed by many witnesses. It is through the Spirit of God that we feel God's presence within, and the Christian life is given a special tangibility. Therefore, it is vital for us to understand the Spirit of God.

On the very first page of the Bible in Genesis 1:1-2, we read "In the beginning God created the heaven and the earth, and the earth was without form and void; and darkness was upon the face of the deep. And the Spirit of God moved upon the face of the waters".

Immediately, there is a dynamic presence of God. The Spirit of God showing action, which brought about a calmness where there was chaos. The Spirit of God was a descriptive moving part of God the Father and God the Son. God does not consist of parts nor can He be divided into parts. The unity of God meaning there is but one God and that the divine nature is undivided and indivisible. The is one God, is the great truth of the Old Testament (Duet. 4:35, 39; I Kings 8:60; Isa. 45:5). The same truth is taught in the New Testament.

The doctrine of the Trinity is not the primary theme, but it would be impossible not to refer to it. We cannot ignore it, because of the Spirit's activity, life, and relationship to God, Himself. The term Trinity, in respect to God the Father, God the Son, and God the Holy Spirit is not found in the Bible, but their threefoldness is clearly apparent in many passages of Scriptures. An example of this is in the Benediction Paul gave us, "The Grace of Our Lord Jesus Christ, and the love of God and the communion of the Holy Spirit be with you all" (2 Cor. 13:14).

The Doctrine of the Trinity, is not a truth of natural theology, but revelation. Reason may show us the unity of God, but doctrine of the Trinity comes from direct revelation. The Bible presents a progressive revelation of the character and activities of each member of the Trinity. The unfolding of the actuality, and acts of the Holy spirit are found in many references throughout many Scriptures associated with God from Genesis to Revelation.

As we look closely at the work in creation by the Spirit of God, it is revealed that three persons of the Godhead were in action. The biblical words for 'Spirit' (Hebrew rauch, Greek pneuma are terms used for their physical formation and their sound, which conveys a sense of their basic meaning. Spirit is also from the Latin word spiritus, which means a "breath" and in the English word "respiration". So the phrase "Spirit of God" is therefore, the "breath of God".

Acknowledgments

I would like to express my appreciation and thanks to Pastor Delman Howard, Dorothy Wall, Shonda Carson, Colleen Maloney, and my family who provided the needed helpful interaction throughout the entirety of this work.

Rev. Dr. Ida M. Mitchell

Preface

There are many factors, which shape our perspective of Biblical Theology, experience, history, culture, revelation, Scripture, and tradition.

Personally, I take seriously the importance of Scripture because it forms the basis of the Christian proclamation or heralds the proclamation of an event. The crucifixion and resurrection of Jesus and the divine victory over sin and death. The continuation of the Word and the act of God himself. The proclamation of God's saving act in Christ; and the appeal to accept God's gracious act of forgiveness of all sin by God, who alone has been wronged and who alone can forgive. There can be no theology of the Christian gospel, which does not take into account the biblical witness. It is true that the Bible is not the revelation of God; only Jesus Christ is the revelation of the Bible. It is an indispensable witness to God's revelation and is a primary source that says, "It is one important way—by which the community of faith keeps open its access to that primordial revelation on which the community has been founded. By taking seriously the witness of Scripture, we are prevented from making the gospel into private moments of religious ecstasy or into the religious sanctification of the structures of society. The Bible can serve, as a guide for checking the contemporary interpretation of God's revelation, making certain that our interpretation is consistent with the biblical witness.

It is the Bible that tells us that God became man in Jesus Christ so that his kingdom would make freedom a reality for all people. This is meaning of the resurrection of Christ. A person no longer has to be a slave to anybody but rebel against all the principalities and powers, which make our existence subhuman. It is in this light that the Holy Spirit is affirmed as an analysis of God's work in the word.

Scripture is not a guide, who makes our decisions for us; it is a theological source because of his power to "renew for us the disclosure of revelation". The Holy Spirit who is present today in our midst is the same God who revealed himself in Jesus Christ as witnessed in the Scriptures.

Tradition refers to the theological reflection of the church upon the nature of Christianity from the time of early church to the present day. It is impossible for any student of Christianity to ignore tradition because the New Testament itself is a result of it.

Experience is also a source doing Biblical Theology. Theology focuses on history as a source for its theological interpretation of God's work in the world because divine activity is inseparable from the history of people. It realizes that its existence comes from a community, which looks back on its unique past, visualizes that reality of the future, and then makes decisions about possibilities of the present.

Christian faith revelation is an event, a happening in human history. It is God making himself known to humanity through a historical act of human liberation. Revelation is what God did in the event of Exodus; it is God tearing down old orders and establishing new ones. Throughout the entire history of Israel, to know God what he is doing in human history on behalf of the oppressed of the land.

In the New Testament, the revelatory event of God takes place in the person of Jesus Christ. He is the event of God, telling us who God is by what he does on behalf of the oppressed. For Christian thinking, the man Jesus is the decisive factor in everything we say about God because He is the complete revelation of God.

1

Ruach and Pneuma

A correct understanding of who and how the Holy Spirit carries implications. The Holy Spirit is a person, not a vague force. Thus, He is someone to whom we can and should pray.

The Holy Spirit being fully divine, is to be accorded the same honor and respect that we give to the Father and the Son. It is appropriate to worship Him as we do them. He should not be thought of as in any sense inferior in essence to them, although His role may sometimes be subordinated to theirs.

The Holy Spirit is one with the Father and the Son. His work is the expression and execution of what the three of them have planned together. There is no tension among their persons and activities.

God is not far off. In the Holy Spirit, the Triune God comes close, so close as to actually enter into each believer. He is even more intimate with us now that in the incarnation. Through the operation of the Spirit, he has truly become Immanuel, "God with us".

The Old Testament referenced to the Spirit of God does not easily form a simple pattern. The Spirit spoken of in the Book of Judges, for example, in a very different way from the Psalms. The very term, "Holy Spirit", appears only in two place (Psa. 51:11; Isa. 63:10-11) KJV; and even when all the other ways of speaking or taken in account, they offer a less definite picture that can be traced in the New Testament.

Nevertheless, the Old Testament is the place to begin. Here are the Scriptures which formed the belief and understanding of Jesus and His earliest followers, and which in turn were interpreted afresh in the light of Jesus' own life, death, and resurrection. Here is the indispensable entrance to the world of ideas, memories, and hopes, which lies behind the New Testament itself. Christian theology has increasingly come to recognize illuminating when it is not simply dismissed as an unimportant preface to the New, and when the temptation is resisted to read into it what is really only properly to be found in the New. It has its own light to throw on this theme.

Who or what is the "Holy Spirit"? In the Old Testament, the express "Holy Spirit" is rare, but there are referenced to the "Spirit of God" and the "Spirit of the Lord", which is used of God in Action. God doing something. The Spirit of God is action in Creation (Gen. 1:1, 2; Job 33:4).

What then, does the Old Testament mean by "Spirit"? What does "Spirit" have to do with God? What is the "Spirit of God"? That can best be seen by looking to see how it uses one particular work: ruach. We cannot hear mention every instance and every nuance of meaning, but we can pit out and highlight the main points.

Ruach as "wind" commonly refers to the strong wind of the storm, the raging blast from the desert, like the one that divided the Red Sea at the Exodus (Ex. 14:21) this driving wind is not identical with ruach of God Himself, but its elemental powerful images of divine strength.

Jesus said, "The Holy Spirit is like the wind. The wind bloweth where it listeneth, and thou heareth the sound thereof, but cannot tell whence it cometh, and whither it Goethe, so is everyone that is born of the Spirit" (John 16:13). We cannot capture the wind in the bottle. It is elusive and mysterious but nonetheless real. We see the effects of the wind, tress bending and swaying the breeze, flags rustling. We see the devastating of the fierce hurricanes. We see the ocean and seas become violent in a gale. We are refreshed by a gentle breeze on a summer day, we know the wind is there.

So it is with the Holy Spirit. He is intangible and invisible. But His work is more powerful than the ferocious wind. The Spirit brings order out of chaos (Gen. 1:2) and beauty out of ugliness. He can transform a sin blistered man into a paragon of virtue (Mark 5:8). The Spirit changes people.

Christ and the Apostles repeatedly describe the Holy Spirit as One who possesses divine attributes and perfections (will describe in the deity of the Holy Spirit). Blasphemy against the Holy Spirit is deemed the unforgivable sin (Mark 5:8; John 12:31). Were the Holy Spirit not God, it is extremely unlikely that blasphemy against him would be unpardonable.

Ruach (Spirit) is largely an impersonal concept. It has to do with natural or supernatural strength, force, power and energy. But it could also carry another meaning as applied to influence and moods of a personal kind, or to "Spirits" conceived of as some sense of personal entities. Examples of these are fairly rare in the Old Testament. It is not always easy to draw the (Num. 5:14) mentions "a spirit of jealousy" that "comes upon" a man when he suspects his wife of unfaithfulness, it would seem most natural, at least to modern readers, take this simply as describing his psychological state not the activity of roaming "spirit". The ancient Hebrews, however, like many African villagers today, would not make such a sharp or straightforward distinction as we are familiar with between what is 'in the mind' and what come 'from outside'. It was part of the same view of things that a "spirit" could be described as passing from one person to another. So God promises Moses that He will "take some of the ruach which is upon you and put it upon them" (Num. 11:17) the recipients are the seventy elders while Elisha asks for a 'double portion' of the ruach of Elijah (II Kings 2:9).

This way of thinking appears to be characteristic especially of the older thinking of the Old Testament. God 'sent an evil ruach between Abimelech and the men of Schechem; and the men of evil ruach from the Lord tormented' Saul (Sam. 16:14). (Isa. 45:7) "I make peace and I create evil". And God allowed a 'lying ruach' to deceive the prophets advising Ahab (I Kings 22:22; II Chron. 18:21). In the case of Saul, the arrival of the evil ruach follows the departure of 'the ruach of the Lord': the two are spoken of in similar terms, and are presumable thought of in much the same way. It is significant that all these 'evil spirits' come from God.

The Old Testament, in fact, offers very little by way of demonology, but it can and does use ruach to speak of a good or evil influence coming from God and exerting an impact on the lives of individuals or groups. Here we are in the area of personal activity—not that the ruach is necessarily thought of as 'a person' in our modern sense' it functions at the level of persons to mould their attitudes and behaviors. Closely connected with this in the sense that is still preserved in English when we say that someone is 'in poor spirits', 'high-spirited' or behaving 'in an angry spirit'. Ruach very commonly has this sense, as when Pharoah's ruach is 'troubled' by his dreams (Gen. 41:8).

Just as the thought of ruach as an elemental force or as a personal influence contributes to understanding of the ruach of God, also is this a more personal conception; for it is the conviction of the Old Testament that man's ruach is not something that he possesses simply by himself. It is a gift from God and depends continually on God. So (Psa. 51:10) prays, create within me a clean heart, Oh God, and put a new and right ruach within me. Cast me not away from thy presence, and take not thy holy ruach from me.

Thus far we have been considering the essential meaning of ruach, and in particular, of the ruach of God in the Old Testament. We have seen that it is essentially the power of 'the living God', to use the common Old Testament phrase,

'Not by might, not by power (i.e. human power), but by my ruach, saith the Lord of Hosts' (Zech. 3:6). But, when we proceed to ask what connection there is between the phase 'the ruach of God' and the Christian conception of the Holy Ghost, the answer is not clear. It is easy enough, indeed, to say that, since the Hebrews became rigidly monotheistic before the end of Old Testament time, the phase is simply and solely periphrases for 'God', and that, therefore, there is not connection between the two expressions other than a purely verbal connection. Any yet such a view is not entirely satisfactory, for it fails to do justice to the nature of prophecy.

The use of the words ruach and pneuma provided an instrument for the development and expression of the Christian doctrine of the Holy Spirit. In Psa. 33:6, we read: "By the Word of the Lord were the heavens made, and all the host of them by the ruach of His mount". There is a close connection between the Word of God and the ruach of God, for to utter a word is to bring forth breath". Psa. 33:9, "He spoke and it was done".

According to Ezekiel, the effect of God sending His Spirit would lead believers to walk in statutes, to keep and do His judgments and be saved from all their uncleanliness (Exe. 36:27-29).

The ruach Yahweh in the Old Testament is not a separate, distinct entity; it is God's power—the personal activity in God's will achieving a moral and religious object. God's ruach is the source of all that is alive, of all physical life. The Spirit of God is the active principle that proceeds from God and gives life to the physical world (Gen. 1:7). It is also the source of religious concerns, raising up charismatic leaders, whether judges, prophets, or Kings. "The ruach Yahweh is a term for the historical creative action of the one God which thought it defies logical analysis, is always God's action".

2

The Personality of The Holy Spirit

The personality of the Holy Spirit contains decisive proof of His Godhead. God's word expresses unequivocally that the Holy Spirit is a person. A "person: is a living entity, endowed with understanding and will, being an intelligent and willing agent. So is the Holy Spirit, all elements, which constitute a personality, are ascribed to and found in Him. "As the Father has life Himself, and the Son has life Himself, so has the Holy Spirit: since He is the Author of natural and spiritual life to mankind, which He could not be unless He had life in Himself, and if He must subsist in Himself" (John Gill).

According to Ezekiel, the effect of God sending His Spirit would lead believers to walk in His statutes, to keep and do His judgments, and be save from all their uncleanness (Ezek. 36:27-29).

True personality is made up of distinctive features of elements, known as heart, mind and will. Being able to think, feel, and will, the Spirit has the capacity for fellowship, which is not possible without personality.

The heart is the seat of affection. With it we love, we have persons and things. In Romans 15:30, Paul speaks of "the love of the Spirit". Without a heart, comfort is not possible. Grief is also an element of the heart. Where there is no love, there is no grief. The Spirit can be grieved (Eph. 4:30).

The mind is the source of intelligence, reason, and knowledge. With our minds we think, plan, devise, and comprehend. There is a beautiful precision, thought, order, planned, and intelligence in all His works. The Scriptures prove His perfect mind (Rom. 8:27). The Spirit has a perfect mind of His own, indicating thought, purpose, and decision (I Cor. 2:10,11).

The will of the Spirit—with our will we act, decide, giving expression to our thoughts and feelings. And true personality consists in preserving the balance between the heart, mind, and will.

It was the Spirit who commanded and removed Philip (Acts 8:29,39).

It was the same Spirit who exercised authority over Peter (Acts 10:19,20).

It was the same Spirit who restrained and constrained Paul

It was this Person of sovereign majesty who uses us just as He determines by His own will (I Cor. 12:11).

Personality then, is essential to our conception of the Spirit, notice some of the actions, which are attributed to Him and cannot be the expression of a power or a thing.

> He dwells in believers (John 14:26)
> He teaches; He brings to remembrance (John 14:26)
> He testifies (John 15:26)
> He convicts of sin (John 16:8)
> He guides into all truths; He hears, He speaks, He shows (John 16:13)
> He inspires Scriptures and speaks through it (Acts 1:2, 16: II Peter 1:21)
> He calls to the ministry (Acts 13:2)
> He sends forth His servants (Acts 13:4)
> He forbids certain actions (Acts 16:6,7)
> He intercedes, etc. (Rom. 8:26)

It is also of the highest importance from the practical standpoint that we decide whether the Holy Spirit is merely some mysterious and wonderful power, which we in our weakness and ignorance are somehow to get hold of and use, or a real person, infinitely holy, infinitely wise, infinitely might, who is to get hold of and use us.

It is of the highest importance from the standpoint of experience that the Holy Spirit be known as a person. Thousands of persons can testify to the blessing that has come into their own lives as they have come to know the Holy Spirit, not merely as a gracious influence, but as a real person, just as real as Jesus Christ Himself, an ever present, loving friend, and mighty helper who is not only always by their side but dwells in theirs heart every day and every hour, and who is ready to undertake for them in every emergency of life.

It is fundamental revelation of Scripture that the Holy Spirit is a person in the same sense that God the Father is a person and the Lord Jesus Christ is a person. The Holy Spirit is presented in Scripture as having the same essential diety as the Father and the Son and is to be worshiped and adored, loved and obeyed in the say way as God. To regard the Holy Spirit in any other way is to make one guilty of blasphemy and unbelief. We walk therefore on most holy ground in thinking of the Holy Spirit of God and the truth involved is most sacred and precious.

The personality of the Holy Spirit has been subject to denial and neglect through the centuries of the Christian Church heretic Arius who stirred up a rebellion against the Scriptural teaching concerning the person Christ and the person of the Holy Spirit was only the "exerted energy of God" manifested in the created world. While his view was repudiated at the Nicene Council in 325, it foreshadowed the defection from Scriptural teaching, which was to follow. Socinius and his followers in the sixteenth century held that the Holy Spirit was merely the eternally proceeding energy of God (Socians deny distinct personality of the Holy Spirit; they concede eternity, because they regard the Spirit as the influence of the eternal God). This laid the foundation for modern Unitarians. Variations in the doctrine of the Holy Spirit have been many through the centuries, but the body of conservative and orthodox Christians have regarded the Holy Spirit as a Person according to the revelation given in the Scriptures.

His work affirms His Personality. The most tangible and conclusive for the personality of the Holy Spirit is found in His works. The very character of His works makes it impossible to interpret the Scriptures properly without assuming His personality.

> His work in creation (Gen. 1:2)
> Empowering (Zech. 4:6)
> Teaching (John 16:13)
> Guidance (Isa. 48:16; Rom. 8:14)
> Comforting (John 14:26)
> Prayer (Rom. 8:26)
> Convincing the world of sin, righteousness, and judgment (John 16:8)
> Restraint of sin (Gen. 6:3; Isa. 59:19, 2; Thess. 2:7)

His commands (Acts 8:29; 13:2; 16:7) makes it evident that the Holy Spirit is a true person. A mere influence or emanation does not create, empower, teach, guide, pray, or command. In the history of the church, opponents of the personality of the Holy Spirit have found it necessary also to deny the inspiration and accuracy of the Word of God in order to sustain their teaching.

In normal discourse, personal pronouns such as I, thou, he, and they are used as pronouns. While personification occurs in literate frequently, it is always quite apparent and does not leave the meaning in doubt. Personal pronouns are used of the New Testament, the Greek work pneuma is neuter and would normally take neuter pronoun. However, in several instances, the masculine for the masculine is that the pronouns refer to a person. Relative pronouns are used in the same way in Eph. 1:13-14. These indirect evidences confirm that the Holy Spirit is commonly regarded as a person in the Scripture.

Christians who have an intelligent comprehension of the truth regard the Holy Spirit as an object of their faith. According to the Scriptures it is possible to sin against the Holy Spirit (Isa. 63:10), grieve Him (Eph. 4:30), reverence Him (Ps. 51:11), and obey Him (Acts 10:19-21). It is impossible in the light of these Scriptures to regard the Holy Spirit intelligently without viewing Him as the personal object of faith. This is further confirmed by the baptismal formula in Matt. 28:19 where the Holy Spirit is associated on an equal basis with the Father and the Son, whose personality is generally accepted. Also the apostolic benediction of II Cor. 13:14 indicates an equality of personality of the Trinity.

If we deny the personality of the Holy Spirit, many passages of Scriptures become meaningless and absurd. For example, I Cor. 2:10 says, "But God hath revealed them unto us by His Spirit: for the Spirit searches all things, yea, the deep things of God". This passage sets before us the Holy Spirit, not merely as an illumination whereby we are enabled to grasp the deep things of God, but as a person who Himself searches the deep things of God and reveals to us the precious discoveries He has made.

In Revelation 2:7, "He that an ear, let him hear what the Spirit saith unto the churches; to him that over cometh will I give to eat of the tree of life, which is in the midst of paradise of God". Here the Holy Spirit is set before us, not merely as an impersonal enlightment that comes to our mind, but as a person who speaks out of the depths of His own wisdom whispers into the ear of His listening servant the precious truth of God.

When we real Gal. 4:6 it tells, "And because ye are sons, God hath sent for the Spirit of His Son into your hearts, crying Abba, Father". Here the Holy Spirit is represented as crying out in the heart of the individual believer. He is not merely a divine influence producing in our own hearts the assurance of our sonship but one who cries out in our hearts, who bears witness together with one spirit that are sons of God (Rom. 8:16).

The Holy Spirit is also represented in the Scriptures as one who prays. In Rom. 8:26, "And in like manner the Spirit also helps our infirmities: for we know not how to pray as we ought; but the Spirit makes intercession for us with groanings which cannot be uttered". It is plain from this passage that the Holy Spirit is not merely an influence that moves us to pray in and through us. It is comforting to know that there are two divine persons praying on their behalf. Jesus Christ who is our mediator is constantly making intercession for us, for He who once walked upon this earth is now ascended into heaven. He knows all about our infirmities. He can be touched with feelings of our infirmities. He dwells in the innermost depths of our being and knows our needs even as we do not know them ourselves, and from these depths makes intercession to the Father for us. The position of the believer is indeed one of perfect security with these two divine persons praying for us.

John 15:26, "But when the comforter is come, whom I will sent unto you from the father, even the Spirit of truth, which proceeded from the Father, he shall testify of me". Here the Holy Ghost is set before us as a person who gives testimony to Jesus Christ, not merely as an illumination that enables the believer to testify of Christ, but as a person who Himself testifies. We read in the next verse, "And ye also shall bear witness, because you have been with me from the beginning". The Holy Spirit bearing witness to the world.

We mentioned the Holy Spirit as a teacher, according to John 14:26, "But the Comforter, which is the Holy Ghost, whom the Father will send in my name, he shall teach you all things, and bring all things to your remembrance, whatsoever I have said unto you". Similarly, John 16:12-14 says "I have yet many things to say unto you, but you cannot bear them now. How be it, when he, the Spirit of Truth, is come, he will guide you into all truth: for He shall not speak of Himself; but whatsoever he shall hear, that he shall speak; and he will show you of things to come. He shall glorify me: for he shall receive of mine, and shall show it into you". In the Old Testament, Nehemiah 9:20, "Thou gavest also thy good spirit to instruct them". It is perfectly clear that the Holy Spirit is not merely an illumination that enables us to apprehend the truth, but a person who comes to teach us daily the truth of God.

The Holy Spirit is also represented as the leader and guide of the children of God. In Rom. 8:14, "For as many as are led by the Spirit of God they are the sons of God. "He takes us by the hand and gently leads us in the paths, which God would have us walk.

The Holy Spirit is also described as a person who has authority to command persons in their service of Jesus Christ. Acts 16:6,7 says, "Now when they had gone throughout Phrygia and the region of Galatia, and were forbidden of the Holy Ghost to preach the Word in Asia, after they were come to Mysia, they assayed to go into Bithynia, but the Spirit suffered them not".

In addition to this, the Holy Spirit is represented as the one who is the supreme authority in the church, who calls persons to work and appoints them to office. In Acts 13:2 say, "As they ministered to the Lord, and fasted, the Holy Ghost said, Separate me Barnabas and Paul for the work whereunto I have called them". Acts 20:28, "Take heed therefore unto yourselves, and to all the flock, over which the Holy Ghost hast made overseers, to feed the church of God, which he had purchased with His own blood".

In Matthew 12:31,32 we read, "Wherefore I say unto you, all manner of sin and blasphemy shall be forgiven unto men, but the blasphemy against the son of man, it shall not be forgive unto me. And whosoever speaketh a word against the son of man, it shall be forgiven him? But whosoever speaketh against the Holy Ghost, it shall not be forgive him, neither in the world, neither in the world to come". This verse indicates that the Holy Spirit can be blasphemed against. It is impossible to blaspheme against anything but a person. If the Holy Ghost is not a person, it certainly cannot be a more serious and decisive sin to blaspheme Him than it is to blaspheme the Son of man, our Lord and Savior, Jesus Christ, Himself.

The doctrine of personality of the Holy Spirit is as distinctive of the religion that Jesus taught as the doctrine of the diety and the atonement of Jesus Christ, Himself. So a question is absolutely necessary, do you regard the Holy Spirit as a real person as Jesus Christ, loving and wise and strong, as worthy of your confidence and love and surrender as Jesus Christ Himself?

The Holy Spirit came into this work to be to the disciples of our Lord after His departure, and to us, what Jesus Christ had been to them during the days of personal companionship with them (John 14:16-17).

The apostolic benediction gives the secret of real Christian life, a life of liberty and joy and power and fullness. (II Cor. 13:14) "The grace of the Lord Jesus Christ, and the love of God, and the communion of the Holy Ghost, be with you all".

The names, which are give Him, reveal both His personality and His divinity. He is called:

My Spirit (Gen. 6:3)
The Spirit of God (II Chron. 15:1)
The Spirit of the Lord (Isa. 11:2)
The Breath of the Almighty (Job 32:8)
The Spirit of the Lord God (Isa. 61:1)
The Spirit of your Father (Matt. 10:20)
The Spirit (Acts 16:7)
The Spirit of Christ (Rom. 8:9)
The Spirit of His Son (Gal. 4:6)

Seeing that these three Divine Persons are one, then the Holy Spirit should receive without distinction one or the other of these appellations. His other names also demonstrate His qualities:

He is the Spirit of:

Holiness (Holy Spirit; Psa. 51:11)
Wisdom (Isa. 11:2)
Counsel (Isa. 11:2)
Understanding (Isa. 11:2)
Worship (John 4:23)
Truth (John 14:17)
Comfort (The Comforter; John 14:26)
Life (Rom. 8:2)
Adoption (Rom. 8:15)
Faith (II Cor. 4:13)
Love (II Tim. 1:7)
Might (II Tim 7:)
Sound Judgment (II Tim. 1:7)
Revelation (Eph. 1:17)
Power (the Power of the Holy Ghost; Eph. 3:20; Rom. 15:13)
Eternity (The Eternal Spirit; Heb. 9:14)
Grace (Heb. 10:29)
Glory (I Peter 4:14)

The Spirit should be treated like a Person. He can be:

Lied to (Acts 5:3)
Tempted (Acts 5:9)
Resisted (Acts 7:51)
Grieved (Eph. 4:30)
Outraged (Heb. 10:29)
Called Upon (Ezek. 37:9)

In the original Greek text, the neuter word SPIRIT should be followed by the neuter pronoun. However, contrary to grammatical rules, the pronoun is masculine (e.g., John 16:7, 8, 13, 14, etc.) to emphasize the fact that the Holy Spirit is a Person and not a thing.

3

The Diety of The Holy Spirit

The Scriptures do not limit themselves in emphasizing the personality of the Holy Spirit, and they affirm His divinity in a most positive way. The Holy spirit bears divine names. When He is called "The Spirit of God", that means He is the very person of God. I Corinthians 2:11 clearly states, "For what man knoweth the things of a man, save the spirit of man which is in him? Even so the things of God knoweth no man, but the Spirit of God". So as man and his spirit make one and the same being, so God and His Spirit are only one.

The Spirit possesses DIVINE ATTRIBUTES. In Hebrews 9:14, as "The Eternal Spirit", He is uncreated, and as uncreated is divine. "Eternal means without beginning or ending of existence". So, "The Spirit" proceeds timelessly from the Father and is coeternal with the Father and the Son.

The attributes are qualities of the entire Godhead. They constitute what He is, they are characteristic of his nature. Attributes should not be confused with properties, which are distinctive characteristics of the various persons of the Trinity. Properties are functions, act or acts of the individual members of the Godhead. The attributes are permanent properties. They cannot be gained or lost. Holiness is not an attributes (a permanent, inseparable characteristic) of Adam, but it is of God. God's attributes are essential and inherent dimensions of his very nature.

Our understanding of God is no doubt filtered through our conceptions projected upon him. They are objective characteristic of his name. In every biblical case where God's attributes are described, it is evident they are part of his nature. The attributes of God are not a collection of fragmentary parts, or as something in addition to his essence. God is love, holiness, and power. It does not mean that there is an unknown being or essence completely or exhaustively known. There is and always will be a mystery regarding God.

Omniscience—"The Spirit searcheth all things, yea the deep things of God" (I Cor. 2:10, 11). There is nothing in, and about God, that the Spirit cannot know. Only God can search the depths of God. All that pertains to God, Christ, Satan, man, heaven, and earth is known to the Spirit. He has complete knowledge having infinite awareness, understanding and insight; and is always present in all places at all times.

Omnipresence—The prefix "omni" signifies "all". An omnibus is a vehicle for all kinds of persons. This quality indicates that the possessor has power to be present everywhere at the same time. The Spirit, however, is in all believers everywhere. "Whither shall I go from thy spirit"? (Psa. 139:7-10). The Spirit dwells at the same time in the ears of all believers (John 14:17).

Omnipotence—Only God can do all possible things. The power of the Spirit is the power of God, who is the omnipotent One (Rev. 19:6). Christ cast out demons by the Spirit of God (Matt. 12:28) by "the finger of God" (Luke 11:20). The Arm, Hand, "Finger of God" are titles descriptive of the unlimited power (Micah 3:8; Rom. 15:13-19).

"Not by might nor by power, but by my Spirit, saith the Lord of hosts" (Zech. 4:6). It is in fact the Spirit that creates. "The Spirit of God hath made me" (Job 33:4). Thou sendest forth thy Spirit, they are created" (Psa. 104:30). God is the All Powerful One (Jer. 32:17). There are some things God cannot do is evident from many Scriptures. He cannot lie, sin, deny Himself, or act contrary to His nature (Num. 23:19; I Sam. 15:29; II Tim. 2:136; Bed. 6:18; James 1:13, 17). But apart from these aspects of divine inabilities the work "impossible" is not in God's vocabulary. As the source of power, unlimited power is His, which always operates in harmony with His wisdom and goodness. In all His dealings creation there is the process of a universal plan and the adaptation to personal ends (Jer. 32:17, 18).

God is all powerful and able to do whatever He wills. Since His will is limited by his nature, God can do everything that is in harmony with his perfections.

The Bible clearly teaches the omnipotence of God. The Lord who is called "Almighty" (Gen. 17:1; Rev. 4:8), is said to be able to do all things he proposes (Job 42:2), for with him all things are possible (Matt. 19:26) and nothing is too difficult (Jer. 32:17), He reigns (Rev. 19:6). Repeatedly the believer is urged to trust God in every walk of life on the ground of his creative, preserving, and providential power (Isa. 45:11-13; 46:4; Jer. 32:16-44; Act 4:24-31). To the Christian the omnipotence of God is a source of great comfort and hope, but to the unbeliever so might a God is a warning and a source of fear (I Peter 4:17; II Peter 3:10; Rev. 19:15). Even the demons shudder (James 2:19), for they know that God has power over them (Matt. 2:29). Someday even the strongest and greatest will seek to hide from him (Rev. 6-15:17; Isa. 2:10-21), and every knee will bow at the name of Jesus (Phil. 2:10).

Holiness—God is absolutely separate from and exalted above all his creatures, and he is equally separate from all moral evil and sin. It denotes the perfection of God and all that he is. In God purity of being is before purity of willing or doing. God does not will the good because he is good, nor is the good because God wills it, God's will is the expression of his nature, which is holy.

Three important things should be learned from the fact that God is holy:

a.   There is a chasm between God and the sinner (Isa. 59:1; Hab. 1:13).

Not only is the sinner estranged from God, but God is estranged from the sinner. Before sin came, man and God had fellowship with each other, now that fellowship is broken and impossible.

b.   One must approach God through the merits of another if he is to approach him at all. Man neither possesses nor is able to acquire the sin-lessness, which is necessary for access to God. But Christ has made access to him possible (Rom. 5:2; Eph. 2:18; Heb. 10:19). In God's holiness lies the reason for the atonement, what his holiness demanded, His love provided (Rom. 5:6-8; Eph. 2:1-9; I Pet. 3:18).

c.   We should approach God "with reverence and awe" (Heb. 12:28). A correct view of the holiness of God leads to a proper view of the sinful self, Palms 66:18, John 1:5-7; Job 40:3-5; Isaiah 6:5-7, and in (Luke 5:8) are striking examples of the relations between the two. Humilia-tion, contrition, and confession flow from a scriptural view of God's holiness.

The last consideration arguing for the Diety of the Holy Spirit is his associa-tion with the Father and the Son and a basis of apparent equality. One of the best know evidence is the baptismal formula prescribed in the Great Commissions: "Go therefore and make disciples of all nations, baptizing them in the name of the Father, and of the Son, and of the Holy Spirit" (Matt. 28:19). The Pauline benediction in 2 Cor. 13:14 is another evidence: "The grace of the Lord Jesus Christ and the love of God and the fellowship of the Holy Spirit be will you all". And in I Cor. 12, as Paul discusses spiritual gifts, he coordinates the three mem-bers of the Godhead: (Now there are varieties of gifts, but the same Spirit and there are varieties of service, but the same Lord, and there are varieties of work-ing, but the same God who inspires them in every one)

(vv. 4-6). Peter likewise, in the salutation of his first epistle, links the three together, noting their respective roles in the process of salvation: "(To the exiles of the dispersion) chosen and destined by God the Father and sanctified by the

Spirit for obedience to Jesus Christ and for the sprinkling with his blood" (I Peter 1:2).

4

The Gifts of The Holy Spirit

There are several major areas of the Holy Spirit's working in Old Testament times. First is the creation. "The earth was without form and void, and darkness was upon the face of the deep and the Spirit God was moving upon the face of the waters" (Gen. 1:2). God's continued working with the creation is attributed to the Spirit. Job 26:13, "By His Spirit, He had garnished the heavens, His hand hath formed the crooked serpent". Isaiah looks to future outpouring of the Spirit as a time of productivity within the creation there will be desolation "until the spirit is poured upon us from on high, and the wilderness be a fruitful field, and the fruitful be counted for a forest" (Isaiah 32:15).

The Old Testament prophets testified that their speaking and writing were a result of the Spirit coming upon them. "And when He spoke to me, the Spirit entered into me and set me upon my feet, and I heard him speaking to me" (Ezekiel 2:2; cf. 8:3: 11:1, 24). The Spirit even entered into such unlikely persons as Balaam (Numbers 24:2). As a sign that Saul was God's anointed, the Spirit came mightily upon him, and he prophesied (I Samuel 10:6, 10). Peter confirmed the testimony of the prophets regarding their experience "no prophecy ever came by the impulse of man, but men moved by the Holy Spirit spoke from God" (II Peter 1:21). In addition, the Book of Acts gives witness that the Holy Spirit spoke by the mouth of David (Acts 1:16; 4:25). Since the Holy Spirit produced the Scriptures, they can be referred to as "God-breathed" (II Tim. 3:16). Another example, we read that appointing Bezalel to construct and furnish the tabernacle, God said, "I have filled him with the Spirit of God, with the ability and intelligence, with knowledge, and all craftsmanship, to devise artistic design, to work in gold, silver, and bronze, in setting cutting stones for setting, and in carving wood, for work in every craft" (Exodus 31:3-5). When the temple was rebuilt by Zerubbabel after the Babylonian captivity, there was a similar endowment "Not by might, nor by power, but by my Spirit, says the Lord of Hosts" (Zech. 4:6). Administration also seems to have been a gift of the Spirit. Pharaoh recognized the Spirit's presence in Joseph, and Pharaoh said to his servants, "Can we find such a man at this, in whom is the Spirit of God"? (Genesis 4:38). And Joshua the son on Nun was full of the Spirits wisdom, for Moses had laid his hands upon him so the people of Israel obeyed him, and he did as the Lord had commanded him (Deutoromy 35:9).

In the time of judged, administration by the power and gifts of the Holy Spirit was especially dramatic. The Spirit of the Lord came upon Othniel, and he judges Israel; he went out to war (Judges 3:10). The Spirit of the Lord came upon Gideon and he went out to war (Judges 14:19).

The Spirit is seen not only in dramatic incidents, he was present in Israel's spiritual life. He was referred to as a "good Spirit" Nehemiah 2:20. "Thou gavest thy good Spirit to instruct them, and did not withhold thy manna from their mouth, and gave them water for their thirst". The Psalmist beseeches God: "Let thy good spirit lead me on a level path" (Psalm 143:10).

The foregoing considerations from the Old Testament depict the Holy Spirit as producing the moral and spiritual qualities of holiness and goodness in the person upon whom he comes in or in whom he dwells. In some cases, this eternal working of the Holy Spirit seems to be permanent, in other cases, such as in the Book of Judges, his presence seems to be intermittent and related to a particular or ministry which is to be carried out.

There is within the Old Testament witnesses to the Spirit an anticipation of a coming time when the ministry of the Spirit is to be more complete. Part of this relates to the coming Messiah upon whom the Spirit is to rest in an unusual degree and fashion. Isaiah 42:1-4 and Isaiah 61:1-3, ("The Spirit of the Lord is upon me, because the Lord has anointed me to bring good tidings to the afflicted; he has sent me to bind up the brokenhearted, to proclaim liberty to the captives, and the opening of the prison to those who are bound…"). Jesus quotes the opening verses of Isaiah 61 and indicates that they are now being fulfilled in him (Luke 4:18-21). There is a more generalized promise, however, one who is not restricted to the Messiah. Joel 2:28-29 "And it shall come to pass afterward, that I will pour out my Spirit on all flesh, your sons and daughters shall prophecy, your young men shall dream dreams, and your young men shall see visions. Even upon the menservants and maidservants in those days, I will pour out my spirit. At Pentecost Peter quoted this prophecy, indicating that it had now been fulfilled.

In Jesus' teaching we find an especially strong emphasis upon the work of the Holy Spirit in initiating persons into the Christian life. Jesus taught that the Spirit's activity is essential in both conversion, which from man's perspective is the beginning of the Christian life and regeneration, which from God's perspective is its beginning. Conversion is man's turning to God. It consists of a negative and a positive element, repentance, that is, abandonment of sin, and faith, that is, acceptance of the promises and the work of Christ. Jesus spoke especially of repentance, and specifically of conviction of sin, which is the prerequisite of repentance.

The work of the Spirit is not completed when a person becomes a believer, it is just the beginning. Jesus, said, "Truly, truly, I say to you, he who believes in me will also do the works that I do; and greater works than these will he do, because I go to the Father" (John 14:12).

The Spirit bestows special gifts upon believers within the body of Christ: Romans 12:6-8

Prophecy
Service
Teaching
Exhortation
Liberality
Giving Aid
Acts of Mercy

I Corinthians 12:4-11

Wisdom
Knowledge
Faith
Healing
Working of Miracles
Prophecy
Ability to Distinguish Spirits
Interpretations of Tongues

Ephesians 4:11

Apostles
Prophets
Evangelists
Pastors and Teachers

I Peter 4:11

Speaking
Service

From the doctrine of the Trinity, the persons of the Trinity are inseparable. So for this reason, the person of Christ when in his mother's womb (Luke 1:15) was attended and filled by the Father and the Holy Spirit. As a result of being filled with the Holy Spirit, the human nature of Christ had all the spiritual gifts. It is clear that in the case of the average Christian being filled with the Spirit doe not necessarily mean that all spiritual gifts have been bestowed, but that all human faculties are under the control of the Holy Spirit. In the person of Christ the human nature was perfect and possessed every spiritual gift. Careful distinction must be made between the excellencies of the human nature and the attributes of the divine nature. While both are true of the same person, the work of the Holy Spirit was in relation to the gifts of the human nature. The gifts of teaching, ministering, administering, rulership, evangelism, shepherding the flock, exhortation, and giving as found in the church are all eminently fulfilled in the person and work of Christ, in addition to some of the gifts which were temporary in nature as far as ordinary men are concerned such as the gifts which were temporary in nature as far as ordinary men are concerned such as the gifts of prophecy, miracles, healing, and discerning of spirits. In Christ was manifestation of the fullness of the Holy Spirit as in (John 3:34). These gifts did not arise from the divine nature, nor were the subject to acquirement in time, but Christ possessed every spiritual gift from the moment of conception. In Christ is the supreme illustration of one not only filled with the Spirit but possessing every gift of the Holy Spirit.

The Study of the gifts of the Holy Spirit can be classified in three categories:

GIFTS OF SPEECH

Tongues
Interpretation of Tongues
Prophecy

GIFTS OF REVELATION

Word of Wisdom
Word of Knowledge
Discerning of Spirits

GIFTS OF ABILITY

Faith
Gifts of Healings
Working of Miracles

Romans 12:1; 14:40, is the use of Spiritual Gifts. The varieties of gifts, Romans 12:1-11. The manifestations or gifts of the Spirit have been noticeably absent from the church for many centuries, but in the past 50 years, God has been restoring these features and His restoration has accelerated immensely in the last 20 years. This Charismatic Renewal has invaded every part of the Christian Church, bringing new life and power to the Body of Christ.

But the greats gift of all gifts is John 3:16, the supremacy of all gifts, the Gift of Love. God gave His Son, and the Son gave His life, that we might have life and have it more abundantly. Being the Spirit of God, He manifested all the qualities of love, grace, mercy, and provision (Psalms 103:13). What a promise full comfort and strength, it is the indwelling Spirit is "that of our Father". The pressures and problem of life may be trying, but He who came from the Father for our benefit, and shares the Father's sympathy and power is able to meet our need with His sufficient grace.

The Spirit, as God's blessed Love-gift can be dealt with in this threefold way:

1. He was give by the Father (John 14:16, 26; Acts 1:4). Along with Jesus, He, Himself is an unspeakable gift, without need of money.

2. He was give by Christ (John 15:26). On the Day of Pentecost, the Spirit came as the promised empowering Gift of the ascended Lord.

3. He came on His own initiative (John 16:13). When He the Holy Spirit…Is come. Behind this voluntary advent and activities of the Spirit.

5

The Symbols of The Holy Spirit

Down to earth illustration can often clarify hard to understand subjects. So Jesus compared himself to a door, a street, a piece of bread, a cup of water, the wind, the rain, fire, salt, oil, and a dove. He likened the kingdom of God to pearl, a fish, net, a supper, a tree, a seed, and a hidden treasure. Paul illustrated his deep theology with referenced to stars, the foundation of a house, the parts of the body, light and darkness, hay and jewels.

Likewise, it is possible to make the truths concerning the Holy Spirit more intelligible to us earthbound mortals. He is invisible Spirit and an incomprehensible God, and for these reasons it is difficult to define his person and his work. But God knows our weaknesses, and therefore in His Word, He employs symbols which are visible signs for and invisible reality. By observing the Biblical use of these symbols, it is possible to come to a riper insight into many aspects of the work of the Spirit of God.

In several places, the Bible closely associates the Holy Spirit with water (John 7:37-39; 4:14; Psalms 87:7). Water is one of the most common of symbols used to describe not only the varied ministry of the Holy Spirit, but also the Holy Scriptures. We cannot live without water, or rain. Water is needed to ally thirst, to give beauty to the flowers, and fertility to crops and harvests. It cleanses the Christian spiritually and indicates that He is the source of life.

Most children can understand these illustrations. We know only too well children can play outside and get muddy. They can intentionally or unintentionally, smear mud on their clothes, on their face, and in their hair. But we know that there is one remedy for dirt, that is water. It will remove the mud from their clothes, face and hair, so that all that was dirty will be sparkling clean for a while at least.

This is the imagery which the Bible uses of the regenerating work of the Holy Spirit. It portrays humankind as being figurative dirty, filthy, and polluted because of his sins. The Holy Spirit regenerates the heart and sanctifies the life, so that gradually the polluting sin is conquered and eventually eliminated. In the sense, man is cleansed and purified from his sin, just as the dirty hands and clothes of a little child are cleansed by water.

Thus, Jesus told Nicodemus, "Unless a man is born of water, and of the Spirit, he cannot enter into the Kingdom of God" (John 3:5). It is not easy to determine the meaning of the word water in the instance. It may be a direct emblem of the Spirit, or it maybe a symbol of baptism, which is by water. It would indicate the purification that is signified in baptism, the purification from our sins by the ind-welling Spirit. In either case water is closely associated with the Spirit. And Jesus' meaning is that in order to enter into the Kingdom of Heaven, we must be born of the Spirit, who cleanses us from our sins just as water washes away dirt. This same idea is hinted at in the Psalm 51, when David prays, "Wash me and I will be whiter than snow...Create in me a clean heart, O God...Renew a right Spirit within me...And take not your Holy Spirit from me". Ezekiel uses the same fig-ure of speech when he writes, "And I will sprinkle clean water upon you, and you will be clean from filthiness, and from all you idols will I cleanse you...And I will put my Spirit with you" (Ezekiel 36:25-27). Paul also makes a definite reference to the cleansing power of the Spirit through regeneration when writing Titus, he says that God "saved us" through the parallel of water and the Spirit in these three passages illustrates to us the cleansing power of the regenerating and sancti-fying Spirit. Water is not only useful to cleanse away dirt, but is also necessary for life, whether it be human, animal, or vegetable.

A good spring can bubble and bring forth an abundance of water, so that even after buckets of water have been drawn, the well is still overflowing. A spring on higher ground, as it spills over and downward, will cause greenness of life where ever it goes. In fact, it can turn a dead, barren desert into an oasis, or into the pro-ductive banks of the Nile or into the lushness of southern California. Using this easily observed fact, the Bible describes the Spirit and His influences. Jesus said, "If a man is thirst, let him come to me and drink". Whoever believes in me, as the Scripture has said, "streams of living water will flow from within them. By this he meant, the Spirit" (John 7:37-39). That means the believer will have a life of holiness that will be like rivers of water, namely, the Holy Spirit. He is "the spring of water willing up to everlasting life". As Jesus, the Holy Spirit abides in his life, and causes him to live a life of Holiness. The Spirit acts as a fountain within the Christian from which flow rivers of good works, going out to others, The Holy Spirit produces life.

This is also the meaning of Isaiah when he quotes God as saying "For I will pour water on him that is thirsty, and the dry ground, I will pour my Spirit on you seed, and my blessing on your offspring, and they will spring up among the grass, as willows by the water course" (Isa. 44:3-4). Where over the Holy Spirit comes, there comes life also. He is to a dead soul what water is to desert soil. He produces spiritual life, just as water give physical life to thirsty dry ground.

Thus, water describes a twofold activity of the Spirit, His cleansing and life-giving power. We should ask ourselves if we know the Spirit of Good as water. Are we being cleansed by Him from our sinful habits, and He is a fountain to our soul causing us to bring forth rivers of holiness. "Whosoever drinketh of the water" (John 4:14). Clean water is one of the prime necessities sought to show her how His Holy Spirit, as a Well of Water within her, was her only source of spiritual life and refreshment. The symbol of water is easy to understand. As Living Water, the presence of the Spirit, the heart quenches thirst and produces life where desolation reigned. He, alone, satisfies the soul's deep thirst. The waters of the earth have failed and I am thirsty still. Aspects of water's beneficial usefulness can be traced:

Cleansing (Ezekiel 36:25-27)
Life, Fertility, and Beauty (Ezekiel 47:1-12)
Joy (Isaiah 12:3)

Without the Blood of Calvary, there never would have been the Water of Pentecost. Jehovah said to Moses, "Thou shalt smite the rock, and there shall come water out of it, that the Jehovah said to Moses, "Thou shalt smite the rock, and there shall come water out of it, that the people may drink" (Exodus 17:6). At the Cross, the Rock of Ages was smitten, and at Pentecost, Water flowed out of it (I Cor. 10:4). "There are rivers of living water" (John 17:37-39). There are many mighty rivers covering the earth, and no two of them are alike. Thus, it is with the spiritual rives. In the Spirit, where is water to swim in, a rive that cannot be passed over (Ezekiel 47:1-12).

There are "floods upon the dry ground" (Isaiah 44:3). Even though water may come as a cloudburst, or as an avalanche, it is still water. What a deluge flooded the earth with judgment in Noah's day. Yet a deluge of the Spirit is just as able to flood the earth with blessing (Rev. 21:3). Floods can stand for the superabundance of the Spirit's supply. "He shall come down like rain" (Psalm 72:6). Absence of rain means famine, scarity, and ruin as many hot countries experience. The Church is certainly suffering from spiritual famine, and is in sad need of hearing the sound of the abundance of rain. May the Holy Spirit send the latter rains for He alone can transform the desert, causing it to blossom as the rose (Isaiah 35:1; Joel 2:23).

There are springs. "A will of water springing up" (John 4:14) Springs are not only reservoirs of pure, fresh water, but the source of great rivers. "All springs are in thee" (Psalm 87:7). This is also true of the Spirit who is our "secret source of every precious thing". In Him is a Spring that never ceases to flow. "Spring up, O Well" (Num. 21:17). "I will be as the dew" (Hosea 14:5). Secret, unnoticed through the night and early morn, the dew descends upon the earth and carries out its effective work.

Wind—In Jesus' discourse with Nicodemus, He compares the Spirit not only of water but also of the wind, "The wind blows wherever it pleases. You may hear the sound, but you cannot tell where it comes from or where it is going. So it is with everyone born of the Spirit" (John 3:8).

That the Holy Spirit is the secret of all life and vitality is evident from this forceful symbol describing His activity. As the natural wind is air in motion, so in the spiritual realm. The Spirit is God in Action, hence, the analogy between the circling winds and the movement of the Spirit in the lives of mankind. The wind is invisible, inscrutable, not amendable to human control, but manifest in its effects, and therefore, a fitting emblem of the mysterious work of the Spirit in the work of regeneration as Jesus indicated in His conversation with Nicodemus.

The symbolism is clear. First of all, the way in which the Spirit works in regeneration is mysterious. It cannot be thoroughly understood. He and His operations are invisible. As is the case with the wind one can see the results, but not the actual activity that causes the results. A hurricane rushes toward an island in the Pacific. It moves hundreds of tons of water into mountainous waves. The sterns of great ships are lifted out of the water, only to spank the water as they ascent. Trees are uprooted. Roofs of houses are torn off. The results of the storm are very evident. But no one has ever seen the wind that causes them.

The reception of the Spirit at Pentecost illustrates the same point. That He was there is clear, for the Apostles spoke in tongues and performed many signs and wonders. But the Spirit could not be seen. There was only a symbol of Him, "a sound like blowing of a violent wind" (Acts 2:2). God used the wind as an emblem of the Spirit to indicate, among other things, his invisibility. Luke describes the coming on the Day of Pentecost "as a rushing might wind" (Acts 2:2). Mighty speaks of power, and the Spirit who came to impart power to witness (Acts 1:8), is all powerful in Himself (Micah 3:8). Rushing suggest the approach, the irresistible action of the Spirit. Coming from above, He is sovereign, and is the Wind, the Breath of the Almighty because He is the manifestation of the divine presence and power, and able to energize and the saints in speedy and effective service.

Wind is varied in its manifestations. At times it is a hurricane force, yet can become "soft as the breath of evening". The jailer needed the Spirit's power, as with earthquake power, and it took such a resistless force to save such a hard cruel man (Acts 16:27-31). But no cyclone experience was necessary for Lydia, who heart silently opened to the Lord as a bud in the morning sun (Acts 16:14).

> "The Spirit lifted me up between the earth and the heaven" (Ezekiel 8:3).
> "The Spirit lifted me up, and brought me into the east gate" (Ezekiel 11:1).
> "The Spirit of he Lord fell upon me: (Ezekiel 11:5).
> "The Spirit of the Lord caught away Philip…who was found at Azotus"
> (Acts 8:30, 40)

Acting as a sudden and might wind, the Spirit can control, and do as He deems best with those He desires to use. As with God, He does according to His will, and none can stay His hand saying, "What doest Thou?" No man knoweth the way of the Spirit (Eccl. 11:5).

Very closely related to the symbol of wind is the symbol of breath for the Holy Spirit. Just as wind is an appropriate symbol for the Spirit of God because it is invisible, so is breath a fitting sign for it too is invisible. But the Work breath implies something else besides the invisibility of the Holy Spirit. It is something that comes from inside a person and indicates that there is life within. As the Psalmists say, "You take away their breath, they die, and return to dust" (Ps. 104:29). The Spirit is life-giving. The Bible uses the emblem to show that the Spirit gives life in four different ways. The Spirit gives natural life. Genesis 2:7, with a direct allusion to the Spirits the Scriptures speak of the giving of life to mankind by saying, "God breathed into his nostrils the breath of life". And in Job 33:4, Elihu says, "The Spirit of God has made me, and the breath of the Almighty gives me life".

In addition to natural life, the Spirit also gives spiritual life. In Ezekiel's vision of he dry bones, there is not only a prophecy of the restoration of Israel's political national life, but also a direct reference to spiritual renovation of individual (Ezekiel 37:9, 10).

There is a third way in which this symbol of breath depicts the life-giving activity of the Spirit. After the resurrection when Jesus appeared to the disciples behind doors, He breathed on them and said, "Receive the Holy Spirit" (John 10:22). His physical breathing did not give the disciplines the Holy Spirit, but it was symbolic of it, so that the disciples would be equipped to perform their official duties as apostles: to give and to retain sins by the preaching of the Word and by church discipline Paul says, "All Scripture is God-breathed" (II Tim. 3:16). Therefore, in this fourth sense, breath is a fitting symbol of the Spirit of God. Thus, when you think Scriptural symbol of breath, remember not only the Holy Spirit is invisible, but also His life-giving activity in the creation of natural man, but in the recreation of Spiritual man.

Everyone understands the symbol of fire. Fire is power. It can be seen as it transforms a gasoline storage tank into a flaming inferno. Figuratively, we speak of setting the world on fire with an ideology. At Pentecost when the Spirit descended, there was not only a symbol in the "sound like the blowing of a violent wind", but there was another symbol in "what seemed to be tongues of fire" that came to rest on the heads of each one in the house (Acts 2:3). This was symbolic of the new power that came to the church by the Spirit on that day, just as Jesus had prophesied earlier, "But you shall receiver power, when the Holy Spirit comes upon you". Because of that power of the Spirit, disciples were on fire with the Spirit, they became Christ's "witnesses in Jerusalem, and in all Judea and Samaria and to the ends of the earth" (Acts 1:8).

Fire is also a purifying force. The Bible frequently uses the illustrations of refining metals by fire. Metal ore was put into a refiner's fire, and through the intense heat, the irons and impurities were burned of, so that only metals of the fines and purest qualities remained (Isa. 4:4; Acts 2:3). Fire is a symbol used of the holy presence and character of God (Deut. 4:24; Heb. 12:29), and also of the Word itself (Jer. 4:14; 20:9; 23:29).

Another symbol of the Holy Spirit is oil. The sick were associated with oil (James 5:14), and the Spirit alone can heal bruised hearts. Oil was associated with food, "Fine Flour, and the Spirit in the Oil. Christ's utterance, "I, by the Spirit of God" reveals how the two were mingled together. For the lamps of the sanctuary "pure olive oil" was provided (Ex. 25:6). "Holy Oil alone continually lighted the temple, where God was worshiped and where the person and work of Christ were wholly symbolized The Spirit illuminates and glorifies Christ, before our eyes. He gives us understanding of heavenly truths, and enables us to worship in spirit and in truth (Ex. 27:20, 21; John 16:14: Phil. 3:3).

There is one other feature regarding the use of oil, namely, the pouring of it (Lev. 8:30; 14:17). Blood and oil typify how we, as sinners, were saved and called to serve the living God. Delivered from spiritual leprosy by the blood of the Cross, and then as priests, sanctified by the oil, or power, of the Spirit (Rom. 8:2, 3).

All four Gospels describe the Holy Spirit as descending like a dove on Jesus at his baptism. The Bible does not tell us why the Spirit descended on Jesus in the form of a dove rather than some other bird or object. The dove is known as a symbol of purity, gentleness, harmlessness, and tenderness. Jesus was to say later on: Matt. 10:16, 11:38; II Cor. 10:1. Therefore, to see the Holy Spirit to descend as a dove, would call these characteristics to mind. It is a reminder for us that no one needs to fear to go to Jesus, for He is full of kindness, gentleness, and love.

Matt. 7:16; Gal. 5:22, Paul points out the unregenerate person brings forth fornication, uncleanness, lasciviousness, and the other sins mentioned in verses 19-21, but just as a fruit tree produces fruit, so also the Holy Spirit produces such as in good virtues as love, joy, peace, and patience. If the tree does not bear fruit, Jesus told in a parable, that tree will be cut off, for without fruit, the tree is useless (Luke 13:7). The Father "cuts off every branch in me that bears no fruit (John 15:2), and such branched are picked up thrown into the fire and burned (v.6).

6

The Names and Titles of The Holy Spirit

At least twenty-five different names are used in the Old and New Testament in speaking of the Holy Spirit. By carefully studying him, there is found a wonderful revelation of the person and work of the Holy Spirit.

The simplest name by which the Holy Spirit is mentioned in the Bible is "the spirit". This name is also used as the basis of other names. The Greek and Hebrew words translated mean literally "breath" or "wind". Both thoughts are in the name as applied to the Holy Spirit.

The thought of breath is brought our in John 20:22, "And when he had said this, he breathed on them, and said unto them, Receive ye the Holy Ghost". It is also suggested in Genesis 2:7. "And the Lord God formed man of the dust of the ground, and breathed into his nostrils the breath of life: and man became a living soul". This becomes more evident when this verse is compared with Psalm 104:30, "Thou sendest forth thy spirit they are created: and thou renewest the face of the earth", and Job 33:4. "The Spirit of God hath made me, and the breath of the Almighty hath given me life".

The significance of this name is that the Spirit is the breathing of God. His innermost life going forth in a personal form to quicken. When the Holy Ghost is received, it is the life of God Himself swelling within us. It is overwhelming and awesome to have an eternal being whom we call God dwelling in a personal way in us.

The thought of the Holy Spirit as "the wind" is brought out in John 3:6-8. "That which is born of the flesh is flesh; and that which is born of the Spirit is Spirit. Marvel not that I said unto thee, ye must be born again. The wind bloweth where it goeth so is everyone that is born of the Spirit".

The Spirit of Jehovah, the name is used of the Holy Spirit in Isaiah 11:2, (ASV) "And the Spirit of Jehovah shall rest upon him". The thought of the name is essentially the same as the preceding with the exception that God here is thought of as the covenant God of Israel.

The Holy Spirit is called the Spirit of the Lord Jehovah in Isaiah 61:1-3, (ASV) "The Spirit of the Lord Jehovah is upon, me; because Jehovah hath anointed me to preach good tidings unto the meek; he hath sent me to bind up the broken-hearted, to proclaim liberty to the captives…" The Holy Spirit is here spoken of not merely as the Spirit of Jehovah but as the Spirit of the Lord Jehovah because of the relation in which God Himself is spoken of in this connection—not merely as Jehovah, the covenant God of Israel, but as Jehovah, Israel's Lord as well as their covenant-keeping God.

The Holy Spirit is called the Spirit of the Living God in II Corinthians 3:6, "For as much as ye are manifestly declared to be the epistle of Christ ministered by us, written not in ink, but with the Spirit of God; Not in tables of stone, but in fleshly tables of the heart". The significance of this name is Apostle Paul drawing a contrast between the Word of God written on "tables that are hearts of flesh" (RV) by the Holy Spirit who in this connection is called the Spirit of the Living God.

The Holy Spirit is called the Spirit of Jesus Christ in Philippians 1:19; "For I know that this shall turn to my salvation through your prayer, and the supply of the Spirit of Jesus Christ". The Spirit is not merely the Spirit of the eternal Word but the Spirit of the Word incarnate, not merely the Spirit of Christ but the Spirit of Jesus Christ. It is the man Jesus exalted, and having received of the Father the promise of the Holy Ghost, he hath shed forth this, which ye now see and hear".

The Holy Spirit is called the Holy Spirit of promise in Ephesians 1:13 (RV): "In whom ye also, having heard the word of truth the gospel of your salvation, in whom, having also believed, ye were sealed with the Holy Spirit of promise". The Holy Spirit is the great promise of the Father and the Son. The one thing for which Jesus bid the disciples wait after His ascension before they undertook His work was "the promise of the Father until the coming of Christ was the coming atoning Savior and King, but when Jesus came and died His atoning death on the cross of Calvary and arose and ascended to the right hand of the father, then the second great promise of the Father was the Holy Spirit to take the pace of our absent Lord (Acts 2:33).

The Holy Spirit is called the Spirit of Holiness in Romans 1:4. "And declared to be the Son of God with power, according to the Holy Spirit, emphasizes the essential moral character of the Spirit as holy, but the name of the Spirit of Holiness to others. The perfect holiness He himself possesses He imparts to those who receive Him (cf. I Peter 1:2).

The Holy Spirit is called the Spirit of Judgment in Isaiah 4:4, "When the Lord shall have washed away the filth of the daughters of Zion, and shall have purged the blood of Jerusalem from the midst thereof by the spirit of judgment, and by the spirit of burning". Thee are two names in this passage; the first is the Spirit of judgment. The Holy Spirit is called this because it is His work to bring sin to light, to convict of sin (sc. John 16:7-9). He judges sin.

The Holy Spirit of Burning in Isaiah 4:3, 4. His name emphasizing His searching, refining illuminating, and energizing work. The Holy Spirit is like a fire in the heart in which He dwells; and is fire test, and refines, and consumes, and illuminates, and warms, and energizes, this He also does. It is the cleansing work of the Holy Spirit, which is especially emphasized in (Isaiah 4:3, 4).

The Holy Spirit is called the Spirit of Truth in John 14:17, "Even the Spirit of truth; whom the world cannot receive because it seeth him not, neither knoweth him, but ye know him; for he dwelleth with you, and shall be in you" (cf. John 15:26; 16:13). The Holy Spirit is called the Spirit of truth because it is the work of the Holy Spirit to communicate truth, to impart truth, to those who receive Him. "When he, the Spirit of truth, is come, he shall guide you in all truth: for he shall not speak for Himself; but what things so ever he shall hear, these shall he speak: and he shall declare unto you the things that are to come" (John 16:13).

The Holy Spirit is called the Spirit of wisdom and understanding in Isaiah 11:2. "And the spirit of the Lord shall rest upon him, the spirit of wisdom and understanding, and the spirit of counsel and might, the spirit of knowledge and of the fear of the Lord". It is the work of the Holy Spirit to impart wisdom and understanding to those who receive him. The three names give refer especially to the gracious work of the Holy Spirit in the servant of the Lord, that is Jesus Christ (Isaiah 11:1-5).

The Holy Spirit is called the Spirit of Grace in Hebrews 10:29. "Of how much sorer punishment, suppose ye, shall he be thought worthy, who hath trodden underfoot the Son of God, and hath counted the blood of the covenant, wherewith he was sanctified, and unholy thing, and hath done despite unto the Spirit of Grace"? This name brings out the fact that it is the Holy Spirit's work to administer and apply the grace of God. He Himself is gracious, it is true, but the name means far more than that; it means that the manifold grace of God our experientially.

The Holy Spirit is called the eternal Spirit in Hebrews 9:14. "How much more shall the blood of Christ, who through The Eternal Spirit offered himself without spot to God, purge your conscience from dead words to serve the living God"? The eternity, the diety, and the infinite majesty of the Holy Spirit are brought out by this name.

The Holy Spirit is called the Comforter over and over again in the Scriptures. In John 14:26, "But the Comforter, which is the Holy Ghost, whom the Father will send in my name, he shall teach you all things, and bring all things to your remembrance, whatsoever I have said unto you". And in John 15:26, "But when the Comforter is come, whom I will send unto you from the Father, even the Spirit of truth, which proceedeth from the Father, he shall testify of me".

7

Conclusion

The basic meaning of the Holy Spirit is God present in His world, creating, giving life, sustaining, and guiding. The Holy Spirit is one of the persons in the Christian Trinity, and without Him the essential nature of Christianity would be changed.

The Trinity is possibly the most difficult of our Christian doctrine. It seems to be allusive and hard to grasp. It is a reality that the doctrine of the Trinity originated in experience, not abstract thought. It was first experience, then doctrine. We have experienced God, the Father above us, Jesus Christ the Son in our history, and the Holy Spirit as God in our world and present with us.

The Doctrine of the Trinity, is not a truth of natural theology, but revelation. It not only comes from experience but from direct revelation. The Scriptures present a progressive revelation of the character and activities of each member of the Trinity. The unfolding of the actuality and acts of the Holy Spirit are found throughout the Scriptures associated with God throughout the Old Testament and Jesus throughout the New Testament. We worship God the Father, in the name of Jesus Christ the Son, in the illumination of the Holy Spirit.

In the New Testament we see the Doctrine of the Trinity emerge in the benediction. II Cor. 13:14, "The grace of the Lord Jesus Christ and the love of God and the fellowship of the Holy Spirit be with you all". Also in the baptismal formulas in the Great Commission: baptizing them in the name of the Father, and the Son, and of the Holy Spirit" (Matt. 28:19). It is clearly said again in I Cor. 12:4-6, "Now there are varieties of service, but the same Spirit; and there are varieties of working, but it is the same Lord; and there varieties of working, but it is the same God who inspires them all in every one".

The Holy Spirit is an indispensable person in the Trinity. Without the Holy Spirit, God would be out of touch with us. He would not be present in our world. Without the Holy Spirit, Jesus Christ would be a dim figure far back in our history. It is the Holy Spirit that brings Jesus Christ from a remote past, making him our living contemporary.

God has not gone off and left his creation, neither has God abandoned us. There is no place to go to escape the presence of God. "Whither shall I go from thy spirit? Or whither shall I go from thy presence? If I ascend up into heaven, thou art there: if I make my bed in hell, behold thou art there. If I take the wings of the morning, and dwell in the uttermost parts of the sea; Even there shall they hand lead me, and thy right had shall hold me. If I shall slay, surely the darkness shall cover me; even the night shall be light about me" (Psalm 139:7-11).

The Holy Spirit is God's won presence. The Holy Spirit was a presence with Jesus. "And I knew him not; but he that sent me to baptize with water, the same said unto me. Upon whom thou shall see the Spirit descending, and remaining on him, the same is he which baptized with the Holy Ghost" (John 1:33).

The Holy Spirit was and still is, a presence in the life of the church. At Pentecost the Holy Ghost was given to the church. The Church was to be an instrument of the Holy Spirit. With the Holy Spirit in the church, it was to be as if Jesus had returned to the church. "Now the Lord is the Spirit, and where the Spirit of the Lord is, there is liberty" (2 Cor. 3:17).

The Holy Spirit gave gifts to the early church. These gifts were made to individuals members of the body of Christ. These gifts were to be exercised, not for self-gratification, but "for the common good" (I Cor. 12:7).

The Holy Spirit was active in the creation of the universe. God created essentially by His Word, the Spirit of God is mentioned before the Word is. Genesis 1:2, "The earth was without form and void, and darkness was upon the face of the waters". The Spirit of God brought order out of chaos.

The highest ethical creation of the Holy Spirit is love. Paul wrote the fruit of the Spirit: "But the fruit of the Spirit is love, joy, peace, patience, kindness, goodness; against such there is no law" (Gal. 5:22-23). In I Cor. 12:31, "And I will show you a more excellent way". The 13th Chapter of 1 Corinthians in a chapter of love. Then I Cor. 14:1, "Make love your aim". Love is the greatest virtue above all other virtues.

The Hebrew ruach and the Greek pneuma can mean breath or wind. They are both translated spirit, both are unseen and intangible, yet you can see the signs and feel their presence. Life is associated breath, where there is no life there is death. When God formed man from the dust of the earth, and breathed into his nostrils the breath of life; man became a living soul" (Gen. 1:7).

The supreme and unique life of Jesus Christ: "He was conceived of the Holy Spirit and born of the Virgin Mary" (Matt. 1:18-25; Luke 1:26-35).

God, in giving us the gift of the Holy Spirit, has given us a foretaste of our final salvation, and the gift is a pledge that He will at last bring us to full redemption.

We are still in the age of the Spirit. He will give us hope, quicken the lives of our churches, and make our pulpits powerful.

A correct understanding of who and what the Holy Spirit is carries certain implications. The Holy Spirit is a person, not a force. Thus, he is someone with whom we can have a personal relationship, someone to whom we can and should pray.

The Holy Spirit being fully divine, is to be accorded the same honor and respect that we give to the Father and to the Son. It is appropriate to worship him as we do them. He should not be thought of as in any sense inferior in essence to them, although his role many sometimes be subordinate to theirs.

The Holy Spirit is one with the Father and the Son. His work is the expression and execution of what the three of them have planned together. There is no tension among heir persons and activities.

God is not far off. In the Holy Spirit, the Triune God comes close, so close as to actually enter into each believer. He is even more intimate with us now than in the incarnation. Through the operation of the Holy Spirit he has truly become Immanuel, "God with us".

My Personal Testimony

The Holy Spirit is a teacher and the Word of God is the textbook from which He teaches. Just as any good teacher, the Holy Spirit from time to time gives tests—not that He might give a grade, but that one might discover the areas in which one still need to grow, as well as appreciate how much a person has grown in certain ways. The test God sends are never intended to destroy, neither are they God's purpose of evaluation. He already knows the heart and the outcome of what the test will be. The test is fort personal sake. God wants everyone to know themselves better.

The Apostle Paul painted a vivid picture of the guiding and teaching role of the Holy Spirit: "Now I say that the heir, as long as he is a child, does not differ at all from a slave, though ha is a master of all, but is under guardians and stewards until the time appointed by the Father. Even so we, when were children, were in bondage under the elements of the world. "But when the fullness of time had come, God sent forth His Son, born of a woman, born under the law, to redeem those who were under the law that we might receive the adoption as sons. And because you are sons. God sent forth His Spirit of His Son into your hearts, crying out, "Abba Father". Therefore, you are no longer a slave but a son, and if a son, then an heir of God through Christ" (Gal. 4:1-7).

The Holy Spirit also applies the law to the heart. A person experiences a sense of conviction, an awareness in one's conscience of right and wrong. The Holy Spirit will call to remembrance what the Word of God says, or He will send people into a person's comes to know Jesus Christ, and He continues to do this after one has been saved.

"And I will pray the Comforter, that He may abide with you forever, Even the Spirit of Truth, whom the world cannot receive, because it seeth Him, not neither knoweth Him, but ye know him, for He dwelleth in you" (John 14:16-16).

"But the Comforter, which is the Holy Ghost, whom the Father will send in my name, He shall teach you all things, and bring all things to you remembrance, whatsoever I have said" (John 14:24-25).

Part of what the Holy Spirit does in a person's life is to remind one of the truth one has learned. Part of His role is to give persons an understanding of what we have learned. He imparts God's reasons and purposes, and reveals God's deepest meaning and desires.

The Grace as manifest in the Holy Spirit gives you the want to.

The Holy Spirit has been imparted to us by the Father to helps us obey.

The Holy Spirit gives us courage to obey.

The Holy Spirit has been given a number of descriptive names: The Spirit of Truth, the Counselor, and the Mighty God. The Holy Spirit works in a person's life continually to nudge, prompt, and point us in the right direction. The presence of the Holy Spirit continues to convict persons in an ongoing way, as a means of leading us away from sin and toward the righteousness of God. We fell His prompting and nudging, causing us to make right choices and good decisions; to resist temptations; and to stand strong against evil.

The leading of the Holy Spirit is very practical. Throughout the Scriptures, there are examples of the Lord saying to us, "Do this, do that, go here, go there". The leading of the Holy Spirit is also leading that result in a win-win proposition for all involved.

Galatians 5:22-23 list the qualities of fruit associates with the Holy Spirit: "But the fruit of the Spirit is love, joy, peace, longsuffering, kindness, goodness, faithfulness, gentleness, self-control".

Love. The fruit of the Holy Spirit is first and foremost love. "The love of God is shed abroad in our hearts by the Holy Spirit who was given to us" (Rom.5:5). All the other qualities associated with having the Holy Spirit flow from the presence of God's love.

Joy is love enjoying all of the goodness of God and all the wonders of His creation.

Peace is love resting on the promises of God and expecting the fulfillment of promises in life.

Longsuffering, or patience is love waiting for God to reveal what He desires to reveal.

Kindness is love reacting to the enemies of God.

Goodness is love choosing what is right and good in God's eyes.

Faithfulness is love keeping its worth remaining true to its Source and clinging to its foundation in Christ Jesus.

Index

978-0-595-39928-4
0-595-39928-2

Printed in the United States
58407LVS00003B/247-249